God's Word, For Real

Why the Bible can be Trusted

I. CAROLINE CROCKER, PHD

ISBN   978-1-957970-31-8

Publisher: Rambling Ruminations, Fairfax, VA
Publication date: November 18, 2025

Cover and line drawings were initially generated with ChatGPT but still required editing by GraphixMunna.

Author website: https://ramblingruminations.com

Table of Contents

Why This Book?

Many years ago, my husband and I went to a conference in the often not-so-sunny Vancouver. It was called God's Word Written (GWW).

The topic was the "truthfulness, dependability, and power of the Bible." I figured I probably wouldn't hear anything new, but that it'd just be a good review. Was I ever wrong!

The speakers included Dr. Mike Licona,[1] Dr. Dan Wallace,[2] Dr. David Lyle Jeffrey,[3] and others. We even had a guest appearance by best-selling author, Anglican theologian, and Regent College professor J.I. Packer![4]

The talks were *excellent*, the information was *invaluable*, and the talks were *riveting*. And I was very relieved that the weather improved.

The talks were recorded, but the website is long gone. Because the information was too good to be lost to the annals of time, I decided to use my notes as the basis for this book.

Keep in mind that these chapters aren't a summary of the conference; instead, they include my own thoughts and research. They are my reflections on what I learned, if you like.

Please note that I've included partial or entire Bible verses for your convenience. Unless

---

[1] All about Mike Licona. https://hc.edu/contact/michael-licona/

[2] All about Dan Wallace. https://danielbwallace.com/

[3] All about David Jeffrey. https://www.baylorisr.org/about-baylorisr/distinguished-professors/david-lyle-jeffrey/

[4] About the now-deceased J.I. Packer. https://en.wikipedia.org/wiki/J._I._Packer

otherwise noted, they are from the English Standard Version. I also encourage you to follow up on the footnotes and look up the Bible references for yourself.

Sorting Truth From Spin

When I ran a science nonprofit, I enjoyed what I called "bunk-detecting." Actually, I still do it at times.[5] I love reasoning, using logic, and finding and evaluating evidence—as one would expect from a trained scientist. In the Christian world, we might call that using the gift of discernment.

Therefore, before the airplane even landed in Vancouver, my attention was laser-focused on

---

[5] One of my articles exposing bunk science can be found here. https://ramblingruminations.com/alternative-medicine-not-good-news/

the GWW conference's claim that we can trust what the Bible says is true. After all, how would we even know? It was written a long time ago!

Some believers seem to think we need to close our eyes and block our ears to all challenges. It's called blind faith, and it's totally not my strong point. Do we, as believers, really have to hang our intellects up at the door of the church?

What about the claims that there are contradictions in Scripture, and the Bible was corrupted as it was copied and translated? Or that it makes ridiculous claims that no reasonable person could swallow? Miracles? Resurrection? What??

Is faith faking it until you make it? Or could it be that faith is built on evidence and reason? That we can, gasp, think about it?

Finally, as you read, you'll soon notice that the conference mainly covered the New Testament (N.T.). Does that matter? Well, if we read what Jesus said, he clearly accepted the Old Testament as authoritative (Mt 5:17-18, Jn 10:35). Therefore, if we are

> ...Scripture cannot be broken. (Jn 10:35)

convinced that He is who He claims to be, probably not.

Let's move on and turn to the first question. In our quest to ascertain if the Bible is true, we need to define what truth is.

Join me on this journey, inspired by the work of the scholars who presented at the GWW conference, and see what you think.

What's Truth? Does It Matter?

If you follow the news, you'll be aware that there seem to be many versions of the truth, at least in politics. I'm not going to even try there. Religion is less contentious!

For the sake of being comprehensive, we should begin with philosophical theories about truth (not that I'm a philosopher).

Correspondence theory states that truth occurs when a statement is in accord with the actual state of affairs. That is, if I say my dog is sleeping next to me and she actually is, my statement is true.

Coherence theory defines truth as the consistency of an assertion with a specified set of propositions. So, if I claim to be 21 years old, then I should not have been born in 1975, nor should I have any grandchildren.

Then there is the **pragmatic view** of truth—what's true is what works. For example, gravity is responsible for an object thrown over the side of a high chair hitting the floor.

Doubtless, these definitions are over-simplified to the point of being false, so I'll move on before I get myself in deep water.

What Does the Bible Say?

To understand what God says about truth, I'll start with an assumption: the Bible is trustworthy and true. Don't worry. I'll review this later, but we have to start somewhere. So, what does the Bible say about truth?

First, it says that the pursuit of truth is vital. Truth is incredibly valuable. It's worth more than wealth, pleasure, and time. It will affect our thinking and actions.

> Buy truth, and do not sell it; buy wisdom, instruction, and understanding. (Pr 23:23)

Hey, think about that for a minute!

Could it be that God values truth so much that He doesn't want us to force ourselves to have faith *despite* the evidence? Might He expect us to use the capacity He gave us for reason, and then trust *because* of the evidence? As I was told many years ago, **"If it is true, you can think about it and it will still be true."** Let's think!

God is Truth

In Scripture, we see that not only does God value truth, but He *is the* Truth. For example, Isaiah twice calls the Father the "God of truth" in Isaiah 65:16. In John 14:6, Jesus claims to be "the way, the truth, and the life." In John 15:26, Jesus promises

> so that he who blesses himself in the land shall bless himself by the God of truth, and he who takes an oath in the land shall swear by the God of truth…(Is 65:16)

that the "Spirit of truth" will come to the disciples. These are only a few of the relevant verses; the overwhelming evidence from Scripture is that God (Father, Son, and Holy Spirit) is the ultimate Truth. Unchanging Truth.

The Book of Truth

> But I will tell you what is inscribed in the book of truth: there is none... (Da 10:21)

Throughout the Bible, also known as the book of truth (Da 10:21), we're repeatedly assured that God is the unchanging One, the same yesterday, today, and forever (He 13:8). In fact, the Hebrew word for truth, *emet,* means constancy, firmness, and duration. It would appear that "Truth is that which is consistent with

> For I the Lord do not change... (Mal 3:6)

the mind, will, character, glory, and being of God." Therefore, the ultimate truth does not change.

Truth Can Be Offensive

Today's view of truth is nothing like this. Truth is often considered relative, impossible, or sometimes even offensive. We say this idea is post-modern, but it's nothing new. Throughout the ages, men have rejected (Ro 2:8), distorted (Ac 20:30), opposed (2 Ti 3:8), and ignored the truth. They were even lying in the Garden of Eden!

> ...truth has perished; it is cut off from their lips. (Jer 7:28)
>
> Truth is nowhere to be found...(Is 59:15 (NIV))

Since truth can be defined as what is consistent with God's character, it can also be incredibly inconvenient. Especially to those who would prefer to live according to "whatever feels good as long as it doesn't hurt anyone." The response? Banish it!

Jesus's followers disagree with the world's perspective. Truth is rock solid; it does not change over time, does not accommodate each person, and should not be ignored. In fact, God built our world so that our actions have consequences. One can claim that the brick wall does not exist for me, but running into it will still produce injury.

Jesus is the Truth

Moreover, Jesus considered truth to be of vital importance. The phrase, "I tell you the truth," appears 78 times in the Gospels. There we are told that "grace and truth came through Jesus Christ" (Jn 1:17) and that, through Him, the Truth will set us free (Jn 8:32). That makes sense if Jesus is who He claims to be:

> You will know the truth, and the truth will set you free. (Jn 8:32)

1. the Truth, the Bread of life (Jn 6:35),
2. the Messiah (Mt 16:16),
3. the One who can forgive sin (Mt 9:5),
4. the One who can control the weather (Lk 8:22-25),
5. the One who can give eternal life (Jn 10:28),
6. and the One who existed before Abraham (Jn 8:58).

If Jesus isn't all He claims, then He couldn't be the Truth, but a liar. And, even worse, the truth would not be what Scripture claims it is, since Scripture itself would not be true. Get your head around that! Therefore, assessing the reliability of the Scripture is essential—did Jesus really say all that? If so, did He prove it? We need to know the Truth!

Jesus Christ was either a liar, a lunatic, or He was who He said He was" (CS Lewis, *Mere Christianity*)

Was Jesus Superhuman?

Prove it! How often have you heard a child say this? How many times have you said it?

We constantly hear extraordinary claims. How about, "An apple a day keeps the doctor away." Or, "It doesn't matter what you believe as long as you're sincere." Then, there's my favorite, "If you keep pulling that face, it'll stick that way."

While working in science, I read that a certain treatment helps 100% of people with fibromyalgia, and that hyperbaric oxygen therapy cures traumatic brain injuries. By the way, none of the above is true.

Amazing Claims in the Bible

The Bible also contains some astounding statements. Jesus made several of them. He agreed with Simon Peter that He's the Messiah. Elsewhere, He said He is one with God (Jn 10:30) and the Son of Man who will return (Mk 14:62). And, in a totally politically incorrect move, in John 14:6, Jesus claimed to be the *only* way to the Father.

The people of the time knew exactly what Jesus was saying, which is why they decided to stone Him. **Jesus was claiming to be God** (Jn 10:33). And, unless He is, the words of C.S. Lewis,

Simon Peter replied, "You are the Christ, the Son of the Living God." And Jesus answered him, Blessed are you, Simon Bar-Jonah! For flesh and blood has not revealed this to you, but my Father who is in heaven. (Mt 16:16-17)

I am the way, the truth, and the life. No one comes to the Father except through me. (Jn 14:6)

Oxford and Cambridge professor, theologian, and inventor of Narnia,[6] bear repeating: that would make him crazy or a liar. Evidently, the people then decided He must be a liar. Even in those days, one did not stone people who were considered crazy. Or God, for that matter.

Jesus Proved It

The operative question is: Did Jesus prove He is God? The biblical narrative provides us with some convincing clues. Jesus healed hundreds or thousands of people (Mt 9 records just a few) and raised a couple of dead people (Mt 9:18). He also read people's minds (Mt 9:4, Lk 5:22-23, and more), cast out demons (Mk 9:17-27, Mt 12:22, Lk 8:26-33), and lived a sin-free life (1 Pt 2:22, 2 Cor 5:21), even according to Pontius Pilate (Lk 23:4, Jn 19:4,6).

> For our sake He made Him to be sin who knew no sin, so that in Him we might become the righteousness of God. (2 Cor 5:21)

---

[6] Some of C.S. Lewis's work can be found here.
https://www.cslewis.com/us

And behold, some people brought to him a paralytic lying on a bed. And when Jesus saw their faith, he said to the paralytic, "Take heart, my son, your sins are forgiven." And behold, some of the scribes said to themselves, "This man is blaspheming." But Jesus, knowing their thought, said, "Why do you think evil in your hearts? For which is easier, to say, "Your sins are forgiven,' or to say, 'Rise and walk'? But that you may know that the Son of Man has authority on earth to forgive sins,"—he then said to the paralytic—"Rise, pick up your bed, and go home." And he rose and went home. (Mt 9:2-6)

Jesus both accurately predicted the destruction of the temple, which occurred approximately 40 years after He died (Mt 24:1-2), and fulfilled over 50 prophecies given 700 or so years before He was born (Is 7:14, Mi 5:2, Is 53, Ps 22). That sure *looks* like proof, but only if one assumes that what the Bible says about Jesus's life is true. Is there any other proof? As it happens, yes.

My God, my God, why have you forsaken me? Why are you so far from saving me, from the words of my groaning?...

But I am a worm and not a man, scorned by mankind and despised by the people. All who see me mock me; they make mouths at me; they wag their heads; "He trusts in the Lord; let him deliver him; let him rescue him, for he delights in him!"...

I am poured out like water, and all my bones are out of joint; my heart is like wax; it is melted in my breast; my strength is dried up like a potsherd, and my tongue sticks to my jaws...

For dogs encompass me; a company of evildoers encircle me; they have pierced by hands and feet—I can count all my bones—they stare and gloat over me; they divide my garments among them, and for my clothing they cast lots...

All the ends of the earth shall remember and turn to the Lord, and all the families of the nations shall worship before you. (Verses from Ps 22)

What Others Say

All reputable scholars and historians agree that Jesus existed and was crucified.[7] We don't need to discuss that. There is, of course, much

---

[7] Even Wikipedia says Jesus existed!
https://en.wikipedia.org/wiki/Historicity_of_Jesus

evidence in the Bible. There are also many references to Him in very early non-Christian sources: the writings of the Roman historian Tacitus, the Jewish historian Josephus, a letter by Pliny the Younger, and even a reference by Lucian, a Greek Satirist.

> Nero fastened the guilt…on a class…, called Christians by the populace. Christus, from whom the name had its origin, suffered the extreme penalty during the reign of Tiberius at the hands of…Pontius Pilate… (Tacitus)

The Ultimate Proof

But frankly, **the historical proof that Jesus existed and was crucified still doesn't prove He's God.** Many people lived and were crucified. It's essential to realize that, because Jesus Himself *claimed* to be God, if He cannot *prove* it, then Jesus was a false prophet. The question then is: was He?

According to the Bible, Jesus Himself predicted that He would die and, after three days, rise from the dead (e.g., Mt 12:39-40, Mt 27:62-64, Jn 10:17-18). If your best friend told you this, what would you think? Maybe, "prove it?" More likely, you would try to get him or her some desperately needed help!

For those with open, but not empty, minds (there's a difference), if Jesus managed to pull this off, fulfilling both his own and older prophecies, that would irrefutably prove his deity. If He didn't, then, according to St. Paul, the Christian faith is useless (1 Cor 15:14).

...I lay down my life that I may take it up again. No one takes it from me, but I lay it down of my own accord. I have authority to lay it down, and I have authority to take it up again. This charge I have received from my Father. (Jn 10:17-18)

The Facts So Far

At this point, we need to reason based on what we read in the Bible and what we know of church history. Obviously, we can't rely on non-Christian or allegedly impartial sources to refer to Jesus's resurrection. After all, a person who acknowledges that Jesus rose from the dead and *still* isn't a believer is not someone to take seriously.

So, let's look at the known facts.

1. Jesus lived.

2. Jesus died.

3. The tomb was empty; there was no body.

"Stop," you may say after number 3. "How do you know? Prove it!"

Where's the Body?

To determine if Jesus rose, we must examine the Gospel accounts and consider possible explanations for what they record.

Women!

Initially, the Bible reports that women visited Jesus's tomb and found it empty. Only afterward did Peter and John go and confirm that the body was missing. Because women weren't considered good witnesses,[8] this lends credibility to the report. If this were a fabricated story, the Gospel writers would have altered that inconvenient detail.

Then, in Matthew 28:11-15, we find the Romans and the chief priests conspiring to explain away the empty tomb. Obviously, at any point, it would have been straightforward to stop this troublesome new religious movement by producing the body. No one did. So, what happened to it?

Conjectures

Various theories about where the body might have been stashed have been advanced. They're all pretty hard to believe. The first is the **Mistake Theory**. It says that the women and the disciples may have gone to the wrong tomb. But presumably the guard(s) at the tomb knew where

---

[8] See the end of the second paragraph for the ancient Jewish view of women as witnesses.
https://www.jewishvirtuallibrary.org/witness#

Jesus was buried. Surely, they wouldn't have made a mistake! Since the burial chamber belonged to Joseph of Arimathea, it's unlikely that no one ever figured out where it was.

The **Swoon Hypothesis**, invented in the 18th century and accepted by the Ahmadiyya Muslims, suggests that maybe Jesus only fainted on the cross. Remember that he was flogged the maximum amount allowed by law, nailed through the wrists and feet, and then stabbed in the side, puncturing his heart. It seems highly unlikely that, once inside the nice, cool tomb, He woke up, pushed the stone away, and appeared. Furthermore, He required no medical attention and convinced people that He had risen from the dead. Believing that requires more faith than I have! Unsurprisingly, this theory has been discredited.

Muslims have put forward a **Substitutionary Theory**. Here, they posit that, because the Son of God should not die, Jesus wasn't crucified but was spirited up to Heaven while still alive. The person who died on the cross was an unfortunate substitute. That doesn't explain the pesky, still-empty tomb.

Lies

Finally, some suggest that the tomb was empty because Jesus's body was stolen. We could call this the **Grave Robber Theory.** But why would anyone have done this—what could their motive have been?

Who Cared?

Three groups had a vested interest in Jesus's condition. Two of these found the empty tomb very inconvenient indeed: the Romans and the Jewish leaders.

The Roman soldiers assigned to guard the tomb could well have been put to death for losing the body. Honestly, even sleeping on the job could be

And when they had assembled with the elders and taken counsel, they [the chief priests] gave a sufficient sum of money to the soldiers and said, "Tell people, 'His disciples came by night and stole him away while we were asleep.' And if this comes to the governor's ears, we will satisfy him and keep you out of trouble." (Mt 28:12-14) a capital offense. The guards had absolutely no motive for stealing and hiding Jesus's body. None.

The chief priests and other Jewish leaders wanted to be rid of Jesus, but they also had no reason to steal the body. After all, that would enable his disciples to claim that He had risen. In fact, they would have been very motivated to produce the body. They couldn't, which was very inconvenient. That's why they bribed the Roman guards to say that the disciples stole the body.

That this lie was circulated is attested to by both non-Christian and early Christian sources, including the writings of Justin Martyr (150-155 A.D.), Origen, and Tertullian.

Who Dies for a Lie?

So, did the disciples steal Jesus's body and hide it somewhere? Only a little reflection reveals that this is highly unlikely. First of all, although the disciples did believe in resurrection on the last day, they were thoroughly confused by Jesus's saying he would rise (Mk 9:31). They had no context for thinking someone would come back to life in three days. It was a surprise.

The disciples thought that Jesus was the Messiah. Stealing and hiding their leader's body would be a very disrespectful act.

Furthermore, stealing Jesus's body would mean that later the disciples were knowingly lying when they claimed He rose from the dead. Most of the disciples were martyred. Would they do that for a claim they knew to be a lie? Amazingly, not one of them ever broke ranks.

Nearly 2000 years later, we still don't have evidence that Jesus's body was stolen or hidden. The highest echelons of politicians couldn't keep Watergate a secret; is it likely that the disciples stole the body and no one ever found out? No.

Jesus lived. Jesus died. The tomb was empty; there was no body. Could it be that Jesus Christ actually did rise from the dead, just as He predicted? Is there more evidence?

For [Jesus] was teaching his disciples, saying to them, "The Son of Man is going to be delivered into the hands of men, and they will kill him. And when he is killed, after three days he will rise." But they did not understand the saying and were afraid to ask him. (Mk 9:31-2)

What Did St. Paul Think?

Now, we'll turn to a lecture whose approach was slightly different from what I'd seen before: via St. Paul.

Saul of Tarsus was born a Roman citizen at about the same time as Jesus and features prominently in the N.T. Scriptures. He was an extremely educated and passionate Jew, both by heritage and by faith. In fact, he was a Pharisee who was so convinced that Jesus was a blasphemer and His followers dangerously deluded that he spent his time hunting them down, even approving their deaths.

From Persecutor to Evangelist

Scripture records that Saul dramatically changed his tune after a remarkable encounter with the risen Jesus (Ac 9:1-19). Thereafter, Saul, now commonly known as Paul, traveled around explaining the gospel (the good news of Jesus).

He was beaten, stoned, and thrown in jail for his efforts (2 Cor 11:25), which might have discouraged quite a few of us! Nonetheless, he kept

But Saul, still breathing threats and murder against the disciples of the Lord, went to the high priest and asked him for letters to the synagogues at Damascus, so that if he found any belonging to the Way, men or women, he might bring them bound to Jerusalem. Now as he went on his way, he approached Damascus, and suddenly a light from heaven shone around him. And falling to the ground, he heard a voice saying to him, "Saul, Saul, why are you persecuting me?" And he said, "Who are you, Lord?" And he said, "I am Jesus, whom you are persecuting.... (Ac 9:1-6) on, experiencing a few shipwrecks, writing letters that Jesus's eyewitnesses read, and finally being beheaded as a martyr under Nero.

In his day, Paul undertook several missionary journeys, covering Israel, Syria, Turkey, Greece, Lebanon, Malta, Cyprus, Italy, Macedonia, and Crete—truly remarkable without the aid of a car.

No reputable scholar doubts that **Paul existed**. They also all accept that, initially, Paul zealously persecuted Christians, and that he eventually became a key apostle.

St. Paul's Epistles

We still have 14 letters (epistles) attributed to Paul which explain his views on various topics. Scholars tend to agree that Paul wrote at least 13 of these, and nobody disputes that he authored seven of them. In fact, Paul's letters, which explain the Gospel and were written between 50 and 67 A.D., are now included as Holy Scripture.

But, wait a minute! How do we know when Paul's letters were written? After all, the oldest physical manuscript we have (Papyrus 46) dates back to 175-225 A.D. It contains most of nine letters.

How Do We Know?

Dr. Mike Licona explained that scholars have several methods for determining when an original document was written. These include:

1. Analysis of the language, since language forms change over the years,
2. Being aware of concomitant historical events,
3. Knowing the individual author's writing style (Paul was highly educated and loved run-on sentences, whereas Peter was a fisherman),
4. Analyzing the names of the people mentioned, and
5. Being aware of where the writer lived (Paul used illustrations that would have been very familiar to people in the places where he ministered).

And Jesus [referring to the temple] said to him, "Do you see these great buildings? There will not be left one stone upon another that will not be thrown

Using Number 2, we can be confident that **the original letters were written before 70 A.D.** That's when the temple was destroyed,[9] a catastrophic event that Jesus predicted (Mt 24:1; Mk 13:2). If it had already happened, it would definitely have been mentioned!

Does it matter when Paul wrote the letters? Yes! Because they were written before 70 A.D. and about 17-34 years after the crucifixion, many of the disciples and eyewitnesses of Jesus's life, death, and resurrection were still alive. This meant they could read or hear them. If Paul had his facts or the theology wrong, more than one of them would likely have shouted.

Moreover, because Paul used to be a persecutor, one might expect his letters to undergo intense scrutiny. But

> [None can] replicate the wisdom of the blessed and glorious Paul. When he was with you, he accurately and reliable taught the word of truth to those who were there at the time.
> (Polycarp to the Philippians 3:2)

[9] Regarding the destruction of the temple, https://www.ebsco.com/research-starters/anthropology/roman-destruction-temple-jerusalem

none of the disciples appear to have challenged Paul's theology. In fact, St Peter's disciple, Clement,[10] a contemporary of Paul's, and St. John's disciple, Polycarp, said Paul's letters were authoritative and trustworthy.

Revolutionary Letters

Make no mistake, what Paul wrote was revolutionary. See 1 Corinthians 15. However, we have no records of anyone protesting the apparently outlandish claim that Jesus rose from the dead. And again, no one produced the body.

Paul also masterfully demonstrated that Jesus fulfilled Old Testament prophecy. After all, as a Pharisee, he was familiar with the Scripture (Number 3 above). As an accepted apostle, Paul wrote that Jesus's death set us free from sin, we are saved by grace, and that, by trusting in Jesus, we can be assured of eternal life.

---

[10] Regarding Clement,
https://www.newadvent.org/fathers/1010.htm

> For I delivered to you as of first importance what I also received: the Christ died for our sins in accordance with the Scriptures, that he was buried, that he was raised on the third day in accordance with the Scriptures, and that he appeared to Cephas [Peter], then to the twelve. Then he appeared to more than five hundred brothers at one time, most of whom are still alive, though some have fallen asleep. Then he appeared to James, then to all the apostles. Last of all, as to one untimely born, he appeared also to me. For I am the least of the apostles, unworthy to be called an apostle, because I persecuted the church of God. (1 Cor 15:3-9)

The Eyewitnesses Didn't Object

The disciples, who had lived with Jesus, knew what Paul was teaching (he checked it with them), and none of them disagreed. No one said, "Hey, what's all this about a bodily resurrection? We know it was in spirit only!" Judging by how important the disciples felt the Gospel message was and how little they initially trusted Paul, if Paul had been wrong in 1 Corinthians 15, they would have called him on it. They didn't.

Logical Inferences

From this, we can infer that the good news of Jesus's resurrection isn't a legend that developed over time. It appears in writing and was undisputed by the apostles shortly after Jesus's death. The belief in the resurrection was there at the beginning. It's not the result of a mass hallucination—scientists know that there's no such thing.

It's not even a grief hallucination, which can occur in ~50% of those who experience a death. After all, when on the road to Damascus, Saul wasn't grieving Jesus's death! He rejoiced in it and was searching out Jesus's followers to *kill* them.

And yet, Paul's entire life changed after seeing the risen Lord. His actions and writing have impacted millions, and his letters are included as Scripture. The same happened to all the other disciples (except Judas). Why? Given all the evidence, only one rational explanation springs to my mind. It's true.

1. Jesus lived.
2. Jesus died.

3. The grave was empty.
4. Jesus rose.

Therefore, it is reasonable to conclude, based on compelling evidence, that **Jesus is who He claims to be. He is God.** That is, if the Scriptures are true to the originals.

But how can we be sure that what we have now in the gospels even resembles what Matthew, Luke, John, or Mark wrote? It's been 2000 years! Are the Muslims right? Did the scribes add to, take away from, and miscopy the documents? Read on!

Can We Trust the Translation?

In the previous chapters, I made extensive use of Scripture. And, I have to admit that the Bible I used is an English translation of what's probably an amalgamation of a copy of a copy of what was initially written.

How, therefore, how can anyone believe that what I read

All Scripture is breathed out by God and profitable for teaching, for reproof, for correction, and for training in righteousness. (2 Tim 3:16) and quoted is authoritative? Why do Christians assert that the Bible is the word of God?

Word of God or Word of People?

We know people wrote the Bible. We can even see the personalities of different authors coming through. Paul loved run-on sentences; Luke was highly analytical; John had a temper but was capable of incredible closeness; Fisherman Peter's letters contain grammatical errors. So, how can we claim that the Bible contains the very words of God?

First, remember that doing things in partnership is totally consistent with God's nature. In Creation, God made and sustains the world, but He still expects man to take care of it. Jesus, the Savior and the Messiah, is fully man and fully God. Our conversion is entirely our decision, but it is completely the result of God's calling. Answers to prayer come about through our petition and God's action.

Why would Scripture not be the same, entirely written by people and fully inspired by God? And, if this were the case, that Scripture is the result of a partnership, wouldn't God be capable of protecting His message throughout the various human processes that bring it to us today? We could end this discussion here, but there's more.

Good News and Bad News

Let's begin with the bad news first. We don't have any original manuscripts: nothing in Paul's, Peter's, Luke's, or John's handwriting. Having said that, there are portions of John that date to about 120 A.D.

The good news is that there are many, many copies. According to Dr. Dan Wallace, there are 5,860 Greek manuscripts, averaging 480 pages each. Sixty of these include the entire N.T. There are also ~10,000 Latin manuscripts that date back to the second century, as well as 5,000-10,000 manuscripts in other languages. If one includes references to and quotations from the N.T. found in the writings of church fathers, we reach a staggering 1 million copies.

More bad news: the scribes, who hand-copied the Scriptures, were far from perfect. Even the most closely related manuscripts disagree 6-10 times per chapter. The Greek N.T. contains about 140,000 words, and there are nearly 500,000 variants. That may seem like something worse than bad news.

But think about it. The reason for all those variants is the presence of multiple copies. On average, we have only 15 copies of writings by classical Greek authors from this period, leaving little room for variants. But there are thousands of copies of the N.T. So, there are thousands of variants. Looks like those analyzing old manuscripts won't be unemployed any time soon.

Differences That Matter

Let's end this chapter with more good news. The documented variants in N.T. wording encompass a range of changes, including differences in word order, word omissions, the use of synonyms, word additions, and spelling mistakes.

But, for a variant to matter, it needs to be both:

1. meaningful (it changes the meaning of the text) and
2. viable (it may represent the original meaning of the text).

Apparently, 75% of N.T. variants are copying mistakes, such as misspellings and nonsense errors. After that, most are due to the use of synonyms. Neither of these categories affects the meaning of the text.

Then, we have the variants that are obviously later additions or deletions, where the scribe sought to explain something or leave it out. These are considered not viable.

The result? Only 1 in 500 textual variants is both meaningful and viable.

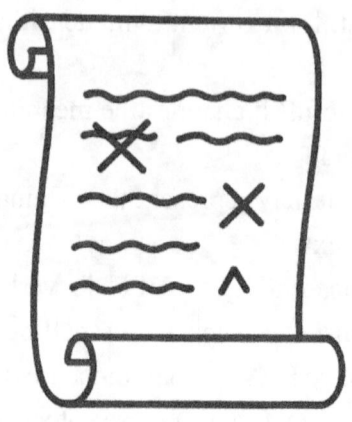

The Worst of the Worst

In this chapter, we will explore an uncomfortable but essential topic. After all, it's vital to know the truth.

So, we turn our attention to the BIG SIX, the most notorious variants contained within the N.T. This is where what's in our Bibles may not be faithful to the original text. Let's explore these meaningful and/or viable variants.

John 5:3-4

The first of the notorious variants is found in John 5, where we are told about Jesus healing a paralyzed man who was lying by a pool at the Sheep Gate. Interestingly, in 1896, a mineral spring was found at that location. So far, so good.

But then, look at the italicized part in the text box. That portion isn't found in the oldest manuscripts. Perhaps some scribe thought insertion of an explanation of the context of the passage was necessary.

Here a great number of disabled people used to lie—the blind, the lame, the paralyzed — *and they waited for the moving of the waters. From time to time, an angel of the Lord would come down and stir up the waters. The first one into the pool after each such disturbance would be cured of whatever disease they had.* (Jn 5:3-4)

But seriously, does the removal of the italicized part change the meaning of the passage? Jesus still healed the man who had been lame for 38 years. So, not really. Whew! One down; five to go.

1 Ti 3:16

I've also italicized the second notorious variant. It's one word. Some manuscripts say "He." Others say "God," and others say "Which." Standard practice in those days was to start a poem with a pronoun, so the

> Great indeed, we confess, is the mystery of godliness: *He* was manifested in the flesh, vindicated by the Spirit, seen by angels, proclaimed among the nations, believed on in the world, taken up in glory. (1 Ti 3:16)

original likely said, "He." Does it matter? Well, who else but Jesus was manifested in the flesh, etc., until He was taken up in glory? This variant doesn't change the meaning of the passage.

Jn 1:18

In the third variant, which also differs by one word, some manuscripts say "the only One" and others "the only Son."

When the Greek is contracted, as was often done, the words for God and for Son only vary by one letter. No doubt this helped create the confusion. However, the "only" part may help explain the passage since the Greek word refers to only produced, created, or begotten.

> No one has ever seen God; the only *God*, who is at the Father's side, He has made him known. (Jn 1:18)

We know from the rest of the N.T. that Jesus is at the Father's side and has made Him known. Therefore, whereas we may not know what the original text said, we have a pretty good idea of what it meant. The variant neither adds to nor detracts from the Scripture message.

1 Jn 5:7-8

This passage was once considered helpful to believers because it served as a proof text for the existence of the Trinity.

The problem is that the italicized part isn't found in early manuscripts. Moreover, it's only found in the margin of the page in half of the later ones. Therefore, although the part about Father, Son, and Holy Spirit is found in the King James Bible, it's not included in more modern translations.

No worries. There's ample evidence for the Trinity throughout the rest of Scripture.[11] No essential doctrines are affected.

> For there are three that testify: *in heaven, the Father, the Word, and the Holy Spirit, and these three are one. And there are three that testify on earth*: the Spirit and the water and the blood; and these three agree. (1 Jn 5:7-8)

Mk 16:9-20

This lengthy text has been used to justify a wide range of weird practices by various churches. But it's a later addition to the chapter, not being found in early manuscripts.

Perhaps an early scribe wondered why the gospel ends so abruptly. Possibly, they surmised that a portion had been lost and decided to fill it

---

[11] In Matthew 28:19, Jesus instructs his followers to go and make disciples and baptize them in the name of the Father, Son, and Holy Spirit.

in. We don't know. But we do know it wasn't there originally.

So, if you have a desire to drink poison or pick up snakes with your hands, you can't justify the practice based on Scripture. Similarly, one cannot use this passage to justify the claim that all believers have the gift of tongues, healing, or exorcism. In my opinion, no loss!

> And these signs will accompany those who believe: in my name they will cast out demons; they will speak in new tongues; they will pick up serpents with their hands; and if they drink deadly poison, it will not hurt them; they will lay their hands on the sick, and they will recover. (Mk 16:17-18)

Jn 7:53-8:11

Now we come to the worst of the worst: the most notorious of all N.T. Scriptural variants. You remember the story about the woman caught in adultery, whom the scribes and Pharisees brought to Jesus? How they tested Him by saying that the Law requires her to be stoned? He told the crowd that those without sin should cast the first stone. When they all slunk away, He  told her He did not condemn her, but that she should sin no more.

Yup. I hate to tell you that textual critics think John 7:53-8:11 is a later addition. The problem is that, although this passage has a ring of authenticity, it pops up in different places in different manuscripts, sometimes after John 21 and sometimes after Luke 21 or Luke 24. It's written in Luke's style and may represent a later addition of a true story. It's totally absent in the earliest manuscripts.

Now, there's no doubt that this stinks. Still, does it change anything? No. Does it make Jesus less merciful or clever? Less our Savior? No. Has any theological principle or essential doctrine

changed? No. Does it change the Gospel message?
No. Breathe a sigh of relief!

Hang on a Minute!

But, wait! We're not yet in the clear. Have
you ever noticed that the description of an incident
in one gospel may differ significantly from the
description of the same incident related in a
different gospel? Or that one gospel may mention
several witnesses, but another only one of them?
Maybe one gospel gives different last words for
Jesus than another. What's with that? Even if we
believe we have reliable copies of what the gospel
writers wrote, how do we know they wrote
accurately? Read on!

Why Do the Gospels Differ?

Have you ever been in a car wreck? If so, the incident probably stands out in your memory as if it happened yesterday. I was in my first accident just after I'd dropped my eldest children off at school. I was taking the youngest to nursery. It was winter in England, when the sun rises late, and it was drizzling.

As I was turning across a lane of traffic, my son asked me why elephants have trunks. He did that kind of thing frequently. Intelligent minds need to know!

Then, seemingly out of nowhere, a gray car, whose headlights were off, ran into the side of my vehicle. That's what I remember.

The report from the person who ran into me was very different. She said she was driving to work along the main road when a car turned right in front of her. She slammed on the brakes but couldn't stop in time. Fortunately, no one was hurt.

Both stories are absolutely true, but they're told from different perspectives and for different purposes. I wanted to justify why I didn't see her; she wanted to show that she wasn't at fault.

It's a Matter of Perspective

Both the purpose and the perspective of the accounting often affect what's written. Imagine you're part of the group of eyewitnesses to Jesus's life who, after His crucifixion, travel around and tell folks about Him and His teachings.

You tell the stories of what Jesus did and said again and again. Those who travel with you find they learn the stories by memory. (Rabbis in N.T. days could memorize 300,000 to 2000,000 words accurately; the average person would have found it easy to memorize 15,000.)

You might write letters to the new churches, encouraging them, sorting out confusion, and laying out doctrine. You also need to ensure that the leaders of the newly formed groups receive the message clearly, resolve disputes, and so on.

Records are Needed

However, as Jesus predicted, not everyone welcomes the new movement with open arms. Persecution begins, and you find that some of those spreading this message die a violent death (~A.D. 60).

It's now imperative that what had been maintained by word of mouth, perhaps because the apostles had limited time, is written down. Thus, the Gospels, or accounts of Jesus's life, came to be.

The Four Accounts

The Gospel of **Mark** has been dated to ~64-70 A.D. and is based on Peter's recollections of, and sermons about, the events of Jesus's life. John Mark, a relative of Barnabus, the son of encouragement, and a scribe mentioned in Acts 12, 13, and 15, penned it. References to Mark can also be found in 2 Timothy 4:11 and Philemon 1:24

The Gospel of **Matthew** was written in ~50-80 A.D., possibly drawing on information supplied by Matthew, the tax collector.

Luke, the physician, is the author of the Gospel of Luke. He's upfront about his sources and the purpose of his book (Lk 1:1-4). It was probably written soon after the Gospel of Matthew.

These three books are called synoptic because they essentially tell the same stories, sometimes even in the same words! Scholars

...it seemed good to me also, having followed all things closely for some time past, to write an orderly account for you, most excellent Theophilus, that you may have certainty concerning the things you have been taught. (Lk 1:3-4)

believe that Mark was written first, and Matthew and Luke were written with a copy of Mark in front of them. And, since the latter two have material not found in Mark, it's possible that they also used a source that has now been lost. Having said that, the gospels are written from different points of view and for various purposes.

The Gospel of **John** was written last (~90-110 A.D.), and there's some doubt about who wrote it. There are also significant differences between John and the first three gospels. Does this matter? Should it cause us to doubt the truth of Scripture?

Remember, if it's true, you can think about it, and it will still be true. So, let's consider the consistencies and contradictions in the gospels. First, notice that four different people wrote the four gospels for four distinct purposes.

Mark for the Romans

Mark was written for use in the evangelism and discipleship of Roman Christians. Thus, John Mark translated many Aramaic expressions into Greek, used Roman time periods, and included several Latin words. He emphasized Jesus's servant nature and compassion. Mark also showed that Jesus was a prophet, priest, and king through the stories of His life. He left his readers to decide, as Jesus asked, "Who do you say that I am?" (Mk 8:27)

According to Mark (and Peter), Jesus is the Son of God. If one accepts that God inspired the Gospel of Mark for the purpose of relating information about Jesus to Roman and Gentile believers, there's no problem with believing it's true.

Matthew for the Jews

Matthew was written in polished or "synagogue" Greek with a different audience in mind: Jews and God-fearers (those who hung around Jews). It also had a distinct purpose: to prove that Jesus is the fulfillment of Old Testament prophecies, establishing Him as the Messiah. Thus, the book is littered with references to the Old Testament and is eminently suitable for teaching Jewish-background believers.

Matthew did not so much catalog the events of Jesus's life as group them around several teaching themes. If one accepts that God inspired the Gospel of Matthew to teach Jewish people about their Messiah, there's no problem believing it's true.

Luke for the Outcasts

Luke begins his book by stating that he has carefully collected and analyzed the accounts written and told by eyewitnesses, and has compiled an orderly account of Jesus's life. This gospel is intended to be a comprehensive narrative, not a collection of teachings or an evangelism and discipleship manual. It was also written from Luke's viewpoint. As a member of the healing profession, Luke had compassion for the sick, the poor, and the outcasts. Thus, he carefully related stories of Jesus's love for Gentiles, lepers, tax collectors, women, and other marginalized groups.

Interestingly, Luke also emphasized Jesus's Jewishness, even though this cultural group usually isolated itself from others. Perhaps he wanted to make the point that Jesus was inclusive and embraced diversity! If one accepts that God inspired the Gospel of Luke to give an orderly and complete account of the events, there's no problem with believing it's true.

John for Everyone

Traditionally, it's held that **John** the Apostle, someone known as a "son of thunder" and "the disciple whom Jesus loved," was the author of the Gospel of

...these are written so that you may believe that Jesus is the Christ, the Son of God, and that by believing you may have life in his name. (Jn 20:31)

John. Some suggest that Lazarus wrote it. Others claim that it, along with 1, 2, and 3 John, was the product of a Johannine school of thought consisting of John's disciples. Regardless of who wrote it, the author told us *why* he wrote it (Jn 20:30-31).

The Odd One Out

The Gospel of John neither presents the incidents in Jesus's life in the same order as the synoptic gospels nor mentions much that we learn in them. Instead, John is highly organized around seven signs or miracles that culminate in the raising of Lazarus, as well as seven "I am" statements and discourses. These culminate in Thomas calling Jesus "my Lord and my God." Known as the "spiritual gospel," John contains several themes, including light vs. dark, belief and faith, and the titles of Jesus.

I am:
The bread of life
The light of the world
The door for the sheep
The good shepherd
The resurrection and the life
The way, the truth, and the life
The true vine

Nonetheless, John's Gospel includes the same general narrative of Jesus's life, showing that Jesus is the Messiah and fulfills Old Testament prophecy, teaches the same principles, and gives the same reasons for Jesus's death and resurrection as the other gospels. If one accepts that God inspired John to show us that Jesus is the Messiah, the Son of God, because, by believing in Him, we will have eternal life, there's no problem with believing it's true.

No Scamming Here!

To some degree, the differences between the accounts make the gospel story more believable—the folks who put the Bible together didn't remove the parts that, at first glance, appear inconsistent. The identical testimony of two witnesses at a car accident would lead us to suspect they had conferred. Similarly, if the stories in the gospels were an exact match and not presented from each person's unique point of view for their own purpose, we might wonder if something was rigged.

Having said that, wouldn't we expect multiple witnesses to at least agree on the basic facts? Like, who went to the tomb and found it empty? Why was Jesus arrested? Who were His ancestors? Or who performed a particular action? How long did Jesus's ministry last? Why do the gospels contain discrepancies concerning these things? Keep reading!

Do Details Really Matter?

Details, details! I'm married to a detail person. When my husband gets home, we have a cup of tea (he's very British) and share our day. That is, I talk, and he listens. He may ask for clarification: who I spoke with (first and last name), where I went (store name at least), when I plan to go again (date and time), and what we're having for dinner (proper and specific names only, please).

My sweet hubby finds it challenging when I say I spoke with the tall lady who's 65 years old, has three children and two grandchildren, wears long dresses, and is struggling with heart disease. Or that we are having food, and it'll be good. I often can't give a specific name, much to his frustration.

For me, the description is much more critical. Perhaps because I spoke three languages as a child, my brain never learned to categorize by words. That explains us in a nutshell.

Discrepancies

Now, what about the Bible? Why are there so many outright discrepancies in the gospels? For example, why is Luke's genealogy of Jesus so very different from that of Matthew?

Who carried Jesus's cross? The synoptic gospels say Simon of Cyrene helped; John does not. What were Jesus's last words? Why do all the gospels differ there?

And then, who found the tomb empty? According to John, Mary Magdalene; according to Matthew, two Marys; according to Mark, three people; and according to Luke, the women and several others.

Once they were at the empty tomb, what did they see? One angel? Two angels? Jesus? These seem like pretty important details, so why the discrepancies?

Old Tyme Writing

Dr. Mike Licona[12] studies Greco-Roman biographies, with an emphasis on Plutarch, who lived from 45 to 120 A.D. and wrote 60 biographies, of which 50 survive to this day. Nine of them are about the same event, but focus on a different character. This made it possible to compare the accounts and look for apparent contradictions. In this way, he learned about writing conventions in Jesus's day.

Unsurprisingly, not only did the ancients not have the Internet, other things were dissimilar, as well. In particular, the standards used for writing a biography were very different from those we utilize today.

---

[12] Here you can see Dr. Licona talking about this himself. https://www.youtube.com/watch?v=of_9mmR6C9c

Ancient biographies were written with a primary goal in mind: to illuminate a character. That is, the author told the story as seemed best for that purpose; a system for accomplishing this was taught to scribes.

Deliberate Actions, not Carelessness

Although our first reaction to the discrepancies in the gospels may be to suspect sloppy workmanship, they're more likely to be the result of the opposite. The gospel writers employed the literary conventions of their time to carefully craft their work and accurately convey Jesus to their readers.

In fact, 90% of the apparent discrepancies can be explained by the use of the following literary customs: adaptation, paraphrase, and simplification.

Adaptation

Adaptation is when one uses words to paint a word portrait, rather than take a word photograph, of the person. The story is composed to reveal the character of the person, to accurately portray more truth about them than can be found in a "photograph."

Take, for example, the apparent discrepancies in Jesus's genealogy. Because of adaptation, only ancestors germane to the author's purpose are included.

Matthew wrote his genealogy, where he includes both Gentile women and Jeconiah (Je 22), from the perspective of Joseph's line. By doing this, Matthew shows that, *through Joseph*, that genealogy does not qualify Jesus to be the Messiah. Matthew then discusses the virgin birth. Problem solved.

In comparison, some scholars believe that Luke starts his genealogy with *Mary.* He wanted to show why Jesus not only could but should be King (Lk 1:30-33).

Paraphrasing

Paraphrasing has been, and remains, another crucial compositional device. In Jesus's day, it would have been considered both acceptable and laudable to create a written portrait by **changing the order of the events**. For example, the stories and discourses in John's Gospel are arranged to illustrate the truths John wished to highlight. An analysis of the composition reveals that the structure, in itself, provides considerable insight into Jesus. Luke does the same thing, only he uses a different order.

Changing the inflection, making a singular into a plural or vice versa, was another common paraphrasing technique. While we might consider it inaccurate, the purposes of the gospel writers were to paint a portrait, not to take a photo.

The use of paraphrasing may explain why the gospels differ with regard to what was written at the top of the cross. We know that the inscription was written in three languages. Perhaps the various gospels provide different reports of what was written because they were translating from other languages. Alternatively, they were paraphrasing. In any case, the idea is the same. The exact wording of the sign is unknown, but we do know that Jesus is the King of the Jews.

Simplification

The final group of literary devices simplify the narrative. There are three simplification techniques: spotlighting, transferal, and compression. Remember that, in Jesus's day, there were no computers, word processors, photocopiers, or even typewriters. Short was good; shorter was better.

Shining a Light

When the gospel writers used **literary spotlighting,** they stuck to what was essential to their story. John only mentioned Mary Magdalene going to the tomb (Jn 20:1). He knew others went, but didn't bother to say it. This can be seen in the very next verse, where Mary says, "*we* don't know where they have laid Him."

Similarly, the various gospels provide different accounts of the number of angels present at the tomb. This may simply be because only one spoke. Matthew and Mark saw no reason to report that a second angel was there since it would add nothing to the portrait being painted.

Transferal

Another simplification technique was **transferal.** That is, it was acceptable to say one person acted when, in fact, it was another, especially if doing so simplified the story. For example, Matthew's Gospel (Mt 8:5-13) tells the story of a centurion who went to Jesus and asked Him to heal his servant. Jesus commended him for his faith and healed the servant. In Luke 7:1-10, we read that the centurion sends someone to ask Jesus to heal his servant, Jesus did, and commended him for his faith.

Matthew just gave the gist of the story; Luke gave us the whole enchilada. Was anything of significance changed? No. The story remains; only the unimportant details have been altered.

Compression

The final simplification technique is **compression**: telling a tale as if it took less time than it did. The use of this device may explain why some gospels seem to suggest that Jesus's ministry lasted approximately one year but Luke details three. The length of time was unimportant; what Jesus did was.

Similarly, in Mark 5, Jairus tells Jesus that his daughter is dying, Jesus sets out to go, and only later do Jairus' servants tell him his daughter is dead. In Matthew 9, Jairus immediately tells the Lord that his daughter is dead.

Which is true? Does it matter? The point is that Jesus went, touched a possibly doubly unclean person (she was both an "adult" female and could, therefore, have been menstruating, and she was dead), and showed He has power over death. (Note that I employed a simplification technique in retelling this story—I didn't mention the interruption by a woman with a flow of blood.)

Keeping the Main Thing the Main Thing

So, the details don't matter? Tell that to my husband! He still doesn't know what we're having for dinner.

What we can know for sure is that **the Scriptures teach us about a Savior who came, died for our sins, and rose again.**

What's Freedom Anyway?

We can hang our lives on the truth of Jesus, and that truth will set us free. But what is freedom?

Free From or Free For?

A Google search for the definition of freedom reveals that it's "the power or right to act, speak, or think as one wants without hindrance or restraint," "the state of not being subject to or affected by," "the power of self-determination attributed to the will," etc. Wow! Did Jesus die so that we all could do as we please, not be subject to anyone, and determine our own futures? This doesn't sound right.

This is because, although the truth of the Bible doesn't change, language and its meanings do. In fact, language is volatile and, to some degree, is becoming more limited due to the use of slang and words borrowed from other languages. Since a person can't contemplate or communicate what they can't articulate, this could have serious consequences for those wishing to understand what the Bible is saying.

"Freedom," for Example

In his lecture, Dr. David Lyle Jeffrey analyzed the meanings of the word "freedom." In the 14th century, "freedom" was defined as "a free spirit, the ability to be generous and self-effacing." Interesting!

Today, "freedom" means the ability to do as you please, but only 700 years ago, "freedom" meant the ability *not* to do as you please. That is, freedom then was about living in a society where a person had certain obligations and enjoyed certain protections. What those were depended on their social status.

...and you will know the truth, and the truth will set you free. (Jn 8:32)

If the Son sets you free, you will be free indeed. (Jn 8:36)

Jesus lived long before the 14th century — what did He mean when He promised that we would be free?

Jesus on Freedom

Fortunately, we don't need to rely on contemporary or even 14th-century definitions of the word "freedom" to understand it. We have the Bible. In John 8, it's stated that by knowing Jesus, we are freed *from* judgment (v. 15), sin (v. 24), punishment (v. 28), and being a slave to sin (v. 34-36). Pretty much, we are free from having to obey the whims of our human nature.

Furthermore, if we do mess up, we are free from having to fear rejection by God and, in the long term, hell. This frees us from fear; we are truly free!

That's not all that Jesus tells us about freedom in John 8. The Truth will also make us free to follow Him (v. 12), hold on to His teaching (v. 31), be a child of God (v. 42), obey Him (v. 51), and know the Messiah of God (v. 58). The chapter is too long to reproduce here, so I recommend that you read it!

We are free to do what is best for us: obey Jesus and live as what we are—children of God. And again, if we mess up, there are consequences here on Earth, but Jesus took the ultimate punishment. That means we are free to repent and return to the One who loved us enough to die for us. That, my friends, is real freedom.

Read the Bible. It's True!

As you see, although the news about our language and culture is bad, it's not hopeless. While it's tempting to take the easy route and flock to hear TV preachers and read books about the Bible rather than the Bible itself, this is not the only option. Nor, in my opinion, is it the one we should choose.

The Lord has provided. The Bible message is trustworthy: the speakers at the GWW conference addressed this topic extensively. Therefore, let's take advantage of what has been provided. Let's study the Bible.

Study Guide for this book is available online at https://ramblingruminations.com/for-discussion/

If you enjoyed this booklet, please leave me a review on Barnes and Noble, Goodreads, or Amazon—or all three!

More to Read

Rev. Dr. Ian Paul, New Testament scholar and
 award-winning blogger with an emphasis
 on Revelation, https://www.psephizo.com

Rev. Aaron Eime, Bible historian specializing in
 the Hebraic roots of Christian faith and
 General Director, CMJ, UK,
 https://www.facebook.com/CMJUK

For answers to specific questions, try:
 https://Bethinking.org

The Bible Project has a wealth of crowd-funded
 resources to help people understand
 Scripture, https://bibleproject.com

Dr. David Lyle Jeffrey, Distinguished Professor of Literature and the Humanities, Baylor University, https://www.baylorisr.org/publications/recent-publications/j-l/jeffrey-david-lyle-publications/

Dr. Michael R. Licona, Professor of New Testament Studies, Houston Christian University, https://www.goodreads.com/author/show/484079.Michael_R_Licona

Dr. Daniel B. Wallace, Executive Director of CSNTM & Senior Research Professor of N.T. Studies at Dallas Theological Seminary, https://danielbwallace.com/